WEAVING SEAMS

Knit: With the **right** side of both pieces facing you and edges even, sew through both sides once to secure the seam. Insert the needle under the bar **between** the first and second stitches on the row and pull the yarn through (**Fig. 5**). Insert the needle under the next bar on the second side. Repeat from side to side being careful to match rows. If the edges are different lengths, it may be necessary to insert the needle under two bars at one edge.

Crochet: With **right** sides facing you, hold edges together. Catch one strand from each edge, being careful to match rows (**Fig. 6**).

Fig. 5

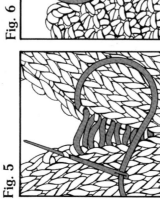

Fig. 6

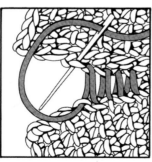

PICKING UP STITCHES

When instructed to pick up stitches, insert the needle from the **front** to the **back** under two strands at the edge of the worked piece (**Figs. 7a & b**). Put the yarn around the needle as if to **knit**, then bring the needle with the yarn back through the stitch to the right side, resulting in a stitch on the needle. Repeat this along the edge, picking up the required number of stitches.

A crochet hook may be helpful to pull yarn through.

Fig. 7a

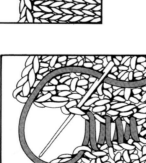

Fig. 7b

FINISHING

Sew one end of a piece of elastic to wrong side of Back corner. Put the Sweater on the dog and place a marker on wrong side of Sweater just forward of back leg. Adjust elastic to fit comfortably and tack in place at marker.

Repeat for other side.

Pink Lady ONLY: Weave ribbon through Eyelet Row.

Grannies ONLY: Weave elastic thread through Neck Edging.

Turtleneck ONLY: Weave elastic thread through middle and bottom of Neck Ribbing.

Basic Crochet, Stripes, and Plaids ONLY: Weave elastic thread through first and last row of Neck Ribbing.

MEASURING YOUR DOG

Take neck and chest measurements (**Fig. 8**). If measurements do **not** match a specific size **exactly,** then go to the largest size that **does** match a measurement and follow the instructions for that size.

Fig. 8

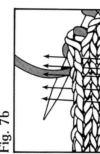

YARN

Yarn amounts in materials are given in ounces only. Please refer to the chart below for grams and yardage. If you are making your sweater longer than length listed, you'll need to purchase additional yarn.

ounces	grams	yards
1	30	65
1½	40	100
2	60	135
2½	70	165
3	90	200
3½	100	230

HOW TO USE THIS BOOK

Once you determine which size you wish to make, find the corresponding size column. Using a pencil, read through the instructions and fill in all the with the numbers that appear on the same li size column. By using a pencil, if you wish t another size later, the numbers can be erased

SIZES

Neck Measurement: _____ "
Chest Measurement: _____ "

1	2	3	4	5	6	7	8	9	10
5	6	8	10	12	14	15	16	17	18
9	10	12	14	16	18	20	22	24	26	28	30

1. Basic Knit

MATERIALS

Worsted Weight Yarn, approximately:

SIZE	1	2	3	4	5	6	7	8	9	10	11	12
Basic – ounces	¾	1	1½	2	2½	3½	4	4½	5	6	6½	7½
Stripes and Bones												
MC (Blue) – ounces	½	¾	1	1¼	1½	2	2¼	2½	2¾	3¼	3½	4
CC (Beige) – ounces	½	¾	1	1¼	1½	2	2¼	2½	2¾	3¼	3½	4
Stripes and Name												
MC (White) – ounces	¾	1	1½	2	2½	3½	4	4½	5	6	6½	7½
Color A (Blue) – ounce	¼	¼	¼	¼	½	½	½	¾	¾	¾	¾	¾
Color B (Red) – ounce	¼	¼	¼	¼	½	½	½	¾	¾	¾	¾	¾
Circular knitting needle, size 8 (5.00 mm) "	16	16	16	16	24	24	24	24	24	24	24	24

Straight knitting needles, sizes 7 (4.50 mm) **and** 8 (5.00 mm) **or** sizes needed for gauge

Double pointed needles, size 7 (4.50 mm)

Marker

Yarn needle

¼" Elastic

Elastic thread

GAUGE: With larger size needles, in Stockinette Stitch, 18 sts and 24 rows = 4"

Note: Increases are made by working into the front **and** into the back of the same stitch.

NECK RIBBING

With smaller size needles, cast on _____ sts **loosely**.

SIZE	1	2	3	4	5	6	7	8	9	10	11	12
cast on sts	24	30	38	48	56	64	70	74	78	84	88	92
ribbing for "	1	1	1	1	1½	1½	1½	1½	2	2	2	2
increasing sts	4	4	2	0	0	0	0	0	0	0	0	2
sts	28	34	40	48	56	64	70	74	78	84	88	92

Work in K1, P1 ribbing for _____ ", increasing _____ sts evenly spaced across last row: _____ sts.

BODY

Change to larger size needles.

Row 1 (Right side): Knit across.

Row 2: Purl across.

Row 3: Increase, knit across to last st, increase: _____ sts.

Working in Stockinette Stitch, continue to increase one st at **each** edge every row, _____ times, ending by working a **purl** row: _____ times, ending by working a **purl** row; then increase every other row _____ more; then increase every other row _____ more: _____ sts.

SIZE	1	2	3	4	5	6	7	8	9	10	11	12
sts	30	36	42	50	58	66	72	76	80	86	90	94
times	6	3	2	0	0	0	0	2	6	7	8	8
more	0	3	5	8	8	9	10	11	9	10	11	14
sts	42	48	56	66	74	84	92	102	110	120	128	138

Leg Openings

Row 1: Knit _____, bind off next _____ sts, knit _____ sts, knit across.

bind off next _____ sts, knit across.

SIZE	1	2	3	4	5	6	7	8	9	10	11	12
Knit	5	5	5	6	7	8	8	9	10	11	12	12
bind off	3	4	5	6	6	7	8	9	9	10	10	10
knit	25	29	35	41	47	53	59	65	71	77	83	89
bind off	3	4	5	6	6	7	8	9	9	10	10	12
measure "	1	1	1	1½	1½	2	2	2½	2½	3	3	3

Note: All three sections of Leg Openings are worked at the same time, using separate yarn for each section.

Row 2: Work across; with second yarn, work across; with third yarn, work across.

Repeat Row 2 until Leg Openings measure approximately _____ ", ending by working a **purl** row.

3

SIZE	1	2	3	4	5	6	7	8	9	10	11	12
add on sts	3	4	5	6	6	7	8	9	9	10	10	12
add on sts	3	4	5	6	6	7	8	9	9	10	10	12
knit across: sts	42	48	56	66	74	84	92	102	110	120	128	138
measures approximately "	4½	5½	6½	7½	8½	9½	10½	11½	12	12½	13	13
Bind off sts	6	6	7	8	9	10	11	12	13	13	14	14
work across: sts	30	36	42	50	56	64	70	78	84	94	100	110
Row 3: sts	28	34	40	48	54	62	68	76	82	92	98	108
Repeat times	5	5	6	7	8	9	10	11	12	13	14	15
sts	18	24	28	34	38	44	48	54	58	66	70	78
measures approximately "	9	11	13	15	17	19	21	22	23	24	25	26
Leg pick up sts	4	6	6	6	8	8	10	10	10	12	12	14
pick up sts twice	4	5	6	6	7	8	9	10	10	11	12	13
place marker: sts	12	16	18	18	22	24	28	30	30	34	36	40

Closing Row: Knit across, add on ___ sts (Figs. 1a & b, page 1), with same yarn, knit across, add on ___ sts, with same yarn, knit across: ___ sts.
Work even until piece measures approximately ___ " from cast on edge or until desired length to end of rib cage, ending by working a purl row.

Shaping

Rows 1 and 2: Bind off ___ sts at the beginning of the next 2 rows, work across: ___ sts.

Row 3 (Decrease row): Slip 1 as if to knit, K1, PSSO, knit across to last 2 sts, K2 tog: ___ sts.

Row 4: Purl across.
Repeat Rows 3 and 4, ___ times: ___ sts.
Work even until Sweater measures approximately ___ " from cast on edge or until desired length to base of tail, ending by working a purl row.
Leave remaining sts on needle.

Weave seam from Neck to Shaping (Fig. 5, page 2).

Back Ribbing
Note: The total number of stitches must be an even number.
With right side facing and circular needle, knit across sts on needle, pick up sts evenly around Back opening (Figs. 7a & b, page 2), place marker.
Work in K1, P1 ribbing around for 1".
Bind off all sts loosely in ribbing.

Leg Ribbing
With first double pointed needle pick up ___ sts, (with next double pointed needle pick up ___ sts) twice, place marker: ___ sts.
Work in K1, P1 ribbing around for 1" (Fig. 2, page 1).
Bind off all sts loosely in ribbing.
Repeat for second Leg Opening.

See **Finishing**, page 2.

4

2. Stripes & Bones to knit

MATERIALS
See Basic Knit, page 3

Work same as Basic Knit in the following Stripe Sequence: Ribbing MC, ★ 14 rows CC, 14 rows MC; repeat from ★ for sequence.

BONES
With CC, add Bones to Sweater using Duplicate Stitch (*Figs. 4a & b, page 1*).
Fold Sweater in half with seam at bottom and find center back.
Beginning at center back on odd numbered MC stripes, follow chart from point A to point B down left side, then from point B to point A down right side.
Beginning at center back on even numbered MC stripes, follow chart from point X to point Y down left side, then from point Y to point X down right side.

See **Finishing**, page 2.

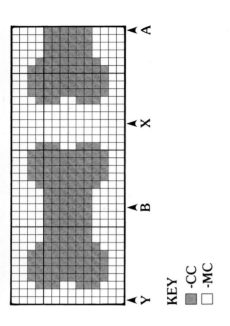

3. Stripes & Name to knit

MATERIALS
See Basic Knit, page 3.

Work same as Basic Knit in the following Stripe Sequence: Ribbing MC, 2 rows MC, 1 row Color A, 1 row Color B, 10 rows MC, ★ 1 row Color B, 1 row Color A, 10 rows MC; repeat from ★ for sequence.

NAME
Using alphabet, chart desired name and mark center of name.
Fold Sweater in half with seam at bottom and find center back.
With Color A and beginning at center of chart, add name to first MC stripe using Duplicate Stitch (*Figs. 4a & b, page 1*).

See **Finishing**, page 2.

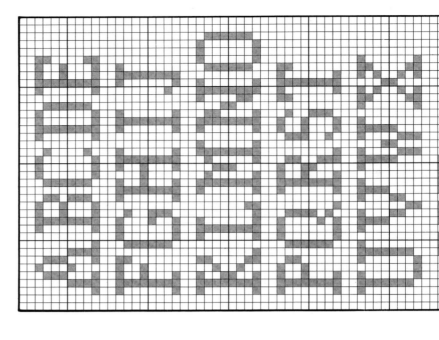

5

4. Rib Tickler to knit

MATERIALS

Worsted Weight Yarn, approximately:

MC (Red) - _____ ounces
Color A (Grey) - _____ yards
Color B (White) - _____ yards

Straight knitting needles, sizes 7 (4.50 mm) **and** 8 (5.00 mm) **or** sizes needed for gauge

_____" Circular knitting needle, size 8 (5.00 mm)

Double pointed needles, size 7 (4.50 mm)

Marker

Yarn needle

¼" Elastic

Elastic thread

GAUGE: With larger size needles, in Stockinette Stitch, 18 sts and 24 rows = 4"

Note: Increases are made by working into the front **and** into the back of the same stitch.

NECK RIBBING

With smaller size needles and MC, cast on _____ sts **loosely**.

Work in K1, P1 ribbing for _____".

BODY

Change to larger size needles.

Row 1 (Right side): With Color A, knit across.

Row 2: Purl across.

Row 3: With Color B, knit across.

Row 4: Purl across.

Row 5: Knit across.

Rows 6 and 7: With Color A, repeat Rows 4 and 5.

Row 8: With MC, purl across increasing _____ sts evenly spaced:
_____ sts.

Working in K1, P1 ribbing, increase one st at **each** edge every row, _____ times;
then increase every other row, _____ times:
_____ sts.

Leg Openings

Row 1: Work across _____,
bind off next _____ sts,
work across _____,
bind off next _____ sts, work across.

Note: All three sections of Leg Openings are worked at the same time, using separate yarn for each section.

Row 2: Work across; with second yarn, work across; with third yarn, work across.

Work even until Leg Openings measure approximately _____", ending by working a **wrong** side row.

Closing Row: Work across, add on _____ sts (*Figs. 1a & b, page 1*), with same yarn, work across, add on _____ sts, with same yarn, work across:
_____ sts.

Work even until piece measures approximately _____" from cast on edge **or** until desired length to end of rib cage.

Continued on page 7.

SIZE	1	2	3	4	5	6	7	8	9	10	11	12
	¾	1	1½	2	2½	3½	4	4½	5	6	6½	7½
	5	6	7	8	9	10	11	12	13	14	15	16
	4	5	6	7	8	9	10	11	12	13	14	15
	16	16	16	16	24	24	24	24	24	24	24	24
	24	30	38	48	56	64	70	74	78	84	88	92
	2	3	3	3	4	4	4	4	5	5	5	5
	4	4	2	0	0	0	0	0	0	0	0	0
	28	34	40	48	56	64	70	74	78	84	88	92
	7	4	3	1	1	1	1	3	7	8	9	9
	0	3	5	8	8	9	10	11	9	10	11	14
	42	48	56	66	74	84	92	102	110	120	128	138
	5	5	5	6	7	8	8	9	10	11	12	12
	3	4	5	6	6	7	8	9	10	10	10	12
	25	29	35	41	47	53	59	65	71	77	83	89
	3	4	5	6	6	7	8	9	9	10	10	12
	1	1	1	1½	1½	2	2	2½	2½	3	3	3
	3	4	5	6	6	7	8	9	9	10	10	12
	3	4	5	6	6	7	8	9	9	10	10	12
	42	48	56	66	74	84	92	102	110	120	128	138
	7	8½	9½	10½	12½	13½	14½	15½	17	17½	18	18

6

SIZE	1	2	3	4	5	6	7	8	9	10	11	12
	6	6	7	8	9	10	11	12	13	13	14	14
	30	36	42	50	56	64	70	78	84	94	100	110
	28	34	40	48	54	62	68	76	82	92	98	108
	5	5	6	7	8	9	10	11	12	13	14	15
	18	24	28	34	38	44	48	54	58	66	70	78
	12	14	16	18	21	23	25	26	28	29	30	31
	4	6	6	6	8	8	10	10	10	12	12	14
	4	5	6	6	7	8	9	10	10	11	12	13
	12	16	18	18	22	24	28	30	30	34	36	40

Shaping
Rows 1 and 2: Bind off ___ sts at the beginning of the next 2 rows, work across:
___ sts.
Row 3 (Decrease row): Slip 1 as if to **knit**, K1, PSSO, work across to last 2 sts, K2 tog:
___ sts.
Row 4: Work across.
Repeat Rows 3 and 4, ___ times:
___ sts.
Work even until Sweater measures approximately ___" from cast on edge **or** until desired length to base of tail.
Leave remaining sts on needle.

Weave seam from Neck to Shaping (*Fig. 5, page 2*).

Back Ribbing
Note: The total number of stitches must be an even number.
With **right** side facing, using circular needle and MC, work in K1, P1 ribbing across sts on needle, pick up sts evenly around Back opening (*Figs. 7a & b, page 2*), place marker.
Work in K1, P1 ribbing around for 1".
Bind off all sts **loosely** in ribbing.

Leg Ribbing
With **right** side facing, using first double pointed needle and Color A, pick up ___ sts, (with next double pointed needle pick up ___ sts) twice, place marker:
___ sts.
Rnd 1: With Color B, knit around (*Fig. 2, page 1*).
Rnd 2: With Color A, knit around.
Rnd 3: With MC, knit around.
Work in K1, P1 ribbing around for 1"
Bind off all sts **loosely** in ribbing.
Repeat for second Leg Opening.

POCKET
With larger size needles and MC, cast on 16 sts **loosely**.
Rows 1-16: Beginning with a **knit** row, work in Stockinette Stitch for 16 rows.
Row 17: With Color A, knit across.
Row 18: With Color B, purl across.
Row 19: Knit across.
Row 20: With Color A, purl across.
Row 21: With MC, knit across.
Ribbing
Work in K1, P1 ribbing for 4 rows.
Bind off all sts **loosely** in ribbing.

Sew Pocket to back of Sweater, using Photo as a guide for placement.

See **Finishing**, page 2.

5. Basic Crochet

MATERIALS

Worsted Weight Yarn, approximately:
- Basic - 9 1/2 ounces
- Stripes
  - MC (Ecru) - 5 1/4 ounces
  - CC (Brown) - 5 ounces
- Turtleneck
  - MC (Rust) - 10 ounces
  - Colors: A, B, C - 3/4 ounce **each**

Crochet hook, sizes F (4.00 mm) **and** H (5.00 mm) **or** sizes needed for gauge
¼" Elastic
Yarn needle
Elastic thread

GAUGE: With larger size hook, 16 dc and 10 rows = 4"

NECK RIBBING

With smaller size hook, ch 8 **loosely**.

Row 1: Sc in back ridge of second ch from hook and in each ch across ***(Fig. 3a, page 1)***: 7 sc.

Row 2: Ch 1, turn; working in BLO ***(Fig. 3b, page 1)***, sc in each sc across.

Repeat Row 2 until 42 ribs (84 rows) are completed.

BODY

Change to larger size hook.

Row 1 (Right side): Ch 3 **(counts as first dc, now and throughout)**; dc in end of first row, dc in end of each row across to last row, 2 dc in last row: 86 dc.

Note: Loop a short piece of yarn around any stitch to mark last row as **right** side.

Row 2 (Increase row): Ch 3, turn; dc in same st and in each dc across to last dc, 2 dc in last dc: 88 dc.

Repeat Row 2, 16 times: 120 dc.

LEG OPENING

First Side

Row 1: Ch 3, turn; dc in next 15 dc, leave remaining dc unworked: 16 dc.

Row 2: Ch 3, turn; dc in next dc and in each dc across.

Repeat Row 2, 5 times.

Finish off.

Center

Row 1: With **right** side facing, skip 12 dc from First Side, join yarn with slip st in next dc; ch 3, dc in next 63 dc, leave remaining dc unworked: 64 dc.

Row 2: Ch 3, turn; dc in next dc and in each dc across.

Repeat Row 2, 5 times.

Finish off.

SIZE	1	2	3	4	5	6	7	8	9	10	11	12
Basic (ounces)	1	1½	2	2½	3¼	4	5	6	6½	7½	8½	9½
Stripes MC (Ecru)	¾	1	1¼	1¾	2	2½	3	3½	4	4¼	4¾	5¼
Stripes CC (Brown)	½	¾	1	1½	1¾	2¼	2¾	3¼	3½	4	4½	5
Turtleneck MC (Rust)	1½	1¾	2	3	4	4½	5½	6	7	8	9	10
Colors: A, B, C	¼	¼	¼	¼	½	½	½	¾	¾	¾	¾	¾
Neck Ribbing: ch	6	6	8	8	8	8	8	8	8	8	8	8
Row 1: sc	5	5	7	7	7	7	7	7	7	7	7	7
Ribs	14	16	18	22	24	28	30	34	36	38	40	42
Rows	28	32	36	44	48	56	60	68	72	76	80	84
Body Row 1: dc	30	34	38	46	50	58	62	70	74	78	82	86
Row 2: dc	32	36	40	48	52	60	64	72	76	80	84	88
Repeat Row 2 (times)	2	2	4	4	6	6	8	8	10	12	14	16
dc	36	40	48	56	64	72	80	88	96	104	112	120
First Side Row 1: dc in next	3	4	5	6	7	8	9	10	11	12	13	15
dc	4	5	6	7	8	9	10	11	12	13	14	16
Repeat Row 2 (times)	1	1	1	3	3	3	3	3	5	5	5	5
Center Row 1: skip	3	4	5	6	7	8	9	9	9	10	11	12
dc in next	21	21	25	29	33	37	41	47	53	57	61	63
dc	22	22	26	30	34	38	42	48	54	58	62	64
Repeat Row 2 (times)	1	1	1	3	3	3	3	3	5	5	5	5

Continued on page 11.

SIZE	1	2	3	4	5	6	7	8	9	10	11	12
	3	4	5	6	7	8	9	9	9	10	11	12
	4	5	6	7	8	9	10	11	12	13	14	16
	1	1	1	3	3	3	3	3	5	5	5	5
	3	4	5	6	7	8	9	9	9	10	11	12
	3	4	5	6	7	8	9	9	9	10	11	12
	36	40	48	56	64	72	80	88	96	104	112	120
	3½	4½	5	6	7	8	9	10	10½	11	11½	11½
	6	7	8	9	10	11	12	14	15	17	18	19
	25	27	33	39	45	51	57	61	67	71	77	83
	26	28	34	40	46	52	58	62	68	72	78	84
	24	26	32	38	44	50	56	60	66	70	76	82
	3	3	4	5	6	7	8	8	9	9	10	11
	18	20	24	28	32	36	40	44	48	52	56	60
	8½	10½	12	14	16	18	20	21	22	23	24	25

Basic Crochet *Continued from page 8.*

Second Side
Row 1: With **right** side facing, skip _9_ dc from Center, join yarn with slip st in next dc; ch 3, dc in next dc and in each dc across: _11_ dc.

Row 2: Ch 3, turn; dc in next dc and in each dc across.

Repeat Row 2, _3_ times.

Closing Row: Ch 3, turn; dc in next dc and in each dc across Second Side, ch _9_ **loosely,** dc in each dc across Center, ch _9_ **loosely,** dc in each dc across First Side.

Chest
Row 1: Ch 3, turn; dc in next dc and in each dc and ch across: _88_ dc.

Row 2: Ch 3, turn; dc in next dc and in each dc across.

Work even until piece measures approximately _10_" from Row 1 of piece **or** until desired length to end of rib cage.

Shaping
Row 1: Turn; slip st in first _14_ dc, ch 3, dc in next _62_ dc, leave remaining dc unworked:

Row 2: Ch 3, [(YO, pull up a loop in next st, YO and draw through 2 loops on hook) twice, YO and draw through all 3 loops on hook **(decrease made)**], dc in next dc and in each dc across to last 3 dc, decrease, dc in last dc: _60_ dc.

Repeat Row 2, _8_ times:

_44_ dc.

Work even until Sweater measures approximately _21_" from Row 1 of Body **or** until desired length to base of tail.

Finish off.

Weave seam from Neck to Shaping **(Fig. 6, page 2).**

Back Edging
With **right** side facing and larger size hook, join yarn with slip st at seam; ch 3, dc evenly across; working in end of rows, dc evenly across; working in last row of Shaping, 5 dc in first dc, dc in next dc and in each dc across to last dc, 5 dc in last dc; working in end of rows, dc evenly across to last row of Chest, dc evenly around to first dc; join with slip st to first dc, finish off.

Leg Edging
Rnd 1: With **right** side facing and smaller size hook, join yarn with slip st in any st; ch 3, working in sts and end of rows, dc evenly around; join with slip st to first dc.

Rnd 2: Ch 3, dc in next dc and in each dc around; join with slip st to first dc, finish off.

Repeat for second Leg Opening.

See **Finishing,** page 2.

11

6. Stripes to crochet

MATERIALS
See Basic Crochet, page 8.

Work same as Basic Crochet in the following Stripe Sequence: Ribbing MC, ★ 2 rows CC, 2 rows MC; repeat from ★ for sequence.

SIZE	1	2	3	4	5	6	7	8	9	10	11	12
	13	13	13	13	17	17	17	17	21	21	21	21
	12	12	12	12	16	16	16	16	20	20	20	20
	14	16	18	22	24	28	30	34	36	38	40	42
	28	32	36	44	48	56	60	68	72	76	80	84
	28	32	38	46	50	58	62	70	74	78	82	86
	28	32	38	46	50	58	62	70	74	78	82	86
	30	34	40	48	52	60	64	72	76	80	84	88
	32	36	42	50	54	62	66	74	78	82	86	90
	34	38	44	52	56	64	68	76	80	84	88	92
	36	40	46	54	58	66	70	78	82	86	90	94
	0	0	1	1	3	3	5	5	7	9	11	13
	36	40	48	56	64	72	80	88	96	104	112	120

MATERIALS
See Basic Crochet, page 8.

NECK RIBBING
With smaller size hook and MC, ch _____ loosely.
Row 1: Sc in back ridge of second ch from hook and in each ch across (*Fig. 3a, page 1*): _____ sc.
Row 2: Ch 1, turn; working in BLO (*Fig. 3b, page 1*), sc in each sc across.
Repeat Row 2 until _____ ribs
_____ rows) are completed.
Finish off.

BODY
Change to larger size hook.
Row 1 (Right side): Join Color A with slip st in end of last row; ch 2, working in end of rows, work _____ hdc evenly spaced across; finish off: _____ hdc.

Note: Loop a short piece of yarn around any stitch to mark last row as **right** side.
Row 2: With **right** side facing, join Color B with slip st in first hdc; ch 2, 2 hdc in same hdc, hdc in next hdc and in each hdc across to last hdc, 2 hdc in last hdc; finish off: _____ hdc.
Row 3: With **right** side facing, join Color C with slip st in same hdc, ch 2, 2 hdc in same hdc, hdc in next hdc and in each hdc across to last hdc, 2 hdc in last hdc; finish off: _____ hdc.
Row 4: With **right** side facing, join MC with slip st in first hdc; ch 3 **(counts as first dc, now and throughout)**, dc in same st, dc in next hdc and in each hdc across to last hdc, 2 dc in last dc: _____ dc.
Row 5 (Increase row): Ch 3, turn; dc in same st and in each dc across to last dc, 2 dc in last dc: _____ dc.
Repeat Row 5, _____ times: _____ dc.
Complete same as Basic Crochet, page 8, beginning with Leg Openings.

Back Edging
Rnd 1: With **right** side facing and larger size hook, join Color A with slip st at seam; ch 2, hdc in each dc across; working in end of rows, hdc evenly across; working in last row of Shaping, 3 hdc in first dc (corner), hdc in next dc and in each dc across to last dc, 3 hdc in last dc (corner); working in end of rows, hdc evenly across, hdc in each dc across; join with slip st to first hdc, finish off.
Rnd 2: With **right** side facing, join Color B with slip st in same st as joining; ch 2, hdc in same hdc and in each hdc across to corner, 3 hdc in corner, hdc in each hdc across to corner, 3 hdc in corner, hdc in each hdc across; join with slip st to first hdc, finish off.
Rnd 3: With Color C, work same as Rnd 2.

Leg Edging
With MC, work same as Basic Crochet.

12

Continued on page 13

SIZE	1	2	3	4	5	6	7	8	9	10	11	12
MC (Grey) ounces	¾	1	1¼	1¾	2	2½	3	3½	4	4¼	4¾	5¼
CC (Cranberry) ounces	½	¾	1	1½	1¾	2¼	2¾	3¼	3½	4	4½	5
	30	34	38	46	50	58	62	70	74	78	82	86
	30	34	38	46	50	58	62	70	74	78	82	86
	32	36	40	48	52	60	64	72	76	80	84	88
	34	38	42	50	54	62	66	74	78	82	86	90

Turtleneck

POCKET
With larger size hook and MC, ch 16 **loosely**.

Row 1 (Right side): Dc in fourth ch from hook and in each ch across: 14 sts.

Note: Place marker to mark last row as **right** side.

Rows 2-6: Ch 3, dc in next dc and each dc across.

Row 7: With **right** side facing, join Color C with slip st in first dc, ch 2, hdc in same dc and in each dc across; finish off.

Row 8: With **wrong** side facing, join Color B with slip st to first hdc, ch 2, hdc in same hdc and in each hdc across; finish off.

Row 9: With **right** side facing, join Color A with slip st in first hdc, ch 2, hdc in same hdc and in each hdc across; finish off.

Sew Pocket to back of Sweater, using Photo as a guide for placement.

See **Finishing**, page 2.

8. Plaids to crochet

MATERIALS
Worsted Weight Yarn, approximately:
MC (Grey) - _____ ounces
CC (Cranberry) - _____ ounces
Crochet hook, sizes E (3.50 mm) **and** G (4.50 mm) **or** sizes needed for gauge
Yarn needle
¼" Elastic
Elastic thread

GAUGE: With larger size hook, in pattern,
16 sts and 16 rows = 4"

NECK RIBBING
With MC, work same as Basic Crochet, page 8.

BODY
Change to larger size hook.

Row 1 (Right side): Ch 1, working in end of rows, work _____ sc evenly spaced across:
_____ sc.

Note: Loop a short piece of yarn around any stitch to mark last row as **right** side.

Row 2: Ch 1, turn; working in FLO, 2 sc in first sc, sc in each sc across to last sc, 2 sc in last sc; finish off: _____ sc.

Row 3: With **right** side facing, join CC with slip st in BLO of first sc; ch 1, sc in BLO of same st, (dc in free loop of sc in row **below** next sc) twice, ★ sc in BLO of next 2 sc, (dc in free loop of sc in row **below** next sc) twice; repeat from ★ across to last sc, sc in BLO of last sc.

Row 4: Ch 1, turn; working in FLO, 2 sc in first sc, sc in each st across to last sc, 2 sc in last sc; finish off: _____ sc.

Row 5: With **right** side facing, join MC with slip st in BLO of first sc; ch 1, sc in BLO of same st, dc in free loop of sc in row **below** next sc, sc in BLO of next 2 sc, ★ (dc in free loop of sc in row **below** next sc) twice, sc in BLO of next 2 sc; repeat from ★ across to last 2 sc, dc in free loop of sc in row **below** next sc, sc in BLO of last sc.

13

SIZE	1	2	3	4	5	6	7	8	9	10	11	12
	36	40	44	52	56	64	68	76	80	84	88	92
	0	0	2	2	4	4	6	6	8	10	12	14
	36	40	48	56	64	72	80	88	96	104	112	120
	4	5	6	7	8	9	10	11	12	13	14	16
	4	5	6	7	8	9	10	11	12	13	14	16
	2	2	2	4	4	4	4	4	6	6	6	6
	3	4	5	6	7	8	9	9	9	10	11	12
	21	21	25	29	33	37	41	47	53	57	61	63
	22	22	26	30	34	38	42	48	54	58	62	64
	2	2	2	4	4	4	4	4	6	6	6	6
	3	4	5	6	7	8	9	9	9	10	11	12
	4	5	6	7	8	9	10	11	12	13	14	16
	2	2	2	4	4	4	4	4	6	6	6	6
	3	4	5	6	7	8	9	9	9	10	11	12
	3	4	5	6	7	8	9	9	9	10	11	12
	36	40	48	56	64	72	80	88	96	104	112	120
	3½	4½	5	6	7	8	9	10	10½	11	11½	11½
	6	7	8	9	10	11	12	14	15	17	18	19
	25	29	33	39	45	51	57	61	67	71	77	83
	26	28	34	40	46	52	58	62	68	72	78	84
	24	26	32	38	44	50	56	60	66	70	76	82
	3	3	4	5	6	7	8	8	9	9	10	11
	18	20	24	28	32	36	40	44	48	52	56	60
	8½	10½	12	14	16	18	20	21	22	23	24	25

Row 6: Ch 1, turn; working in FLO, 2 sc in first st, sc in each st across to last sc, 2 sc in last sc; finish off: ___ sc.

Row 7: With **right** side facing, join CC with slip st in BLO of first sc; ch 1, sc in same st and in next 2 sc, (dc in free loop of sc in row **below** next sc) twice, ★ sc in BLO of next 2 sc, (dc in free loop of sc in row **below** next sc) twice; repeat from ★ across to last 3 sc, sc in BLO of last 3 sc.

Maintaining pattern (working new sts in Plaid pattern), continue to increase one stitch at each edge every other row, ___ times: ___ sts.

LEG OPENINGS

Note: Maintain established pattern throughout.

First Side

Row 1: Ch 1, turn; work across ___ sts, leave remaining sts unworked: ___ sts.

Row 2: Ch 1, turn; work across.

Repeat Row 2, ___ times.

Finish off.

Center

Row 1: With **right** side facing, skip ___ sts from First Side, join yarn with slip st in next st; ch 1, working in same st and in next ___ sts, work across, leave remaining sts unworked: ___ sts.

Row 2: Ch 1, turn; work across.

Repeat Row 2, ___ times.

Finish off.

Second Side

Row 1: With **right** side facing, skip ___ sts from Center, join yarn with slip st in next st; ch 1, work across: ___ sts.

Row 2: Ch 1, turn; work across.

Repeat Row 2, ___ times.

Closing Row: Ch 1, turn; work across Second Side, ch ___ **loosely**, work across Center, ch ___ **loosely**, work across First Side: ___ sts.

Chest

Work even until piece measures approximately ___" from Row 1 of Body **or** until desired length to end of rib cage, ending by working a **right** side row.

Shaping

Row 1: Turn; slip st in first ___ sts, ch 1, sc in same st and in next ___ sts; leave remaining sts unworked: ___ sts.

Row 2 (Decrease row): Ch 1, turn; work decrease as follows: pull up a loop in next 2 sts, YO and draw through all 3 loops on hook, work across to last 2 sts, decrease: ___ sts.

Repeat Row 2, ___ times.

Work even until Sweater measures approximately ___" from Row 1 of Body **or** until desired length to base of tail.

Finish off.

Weave seam from Neck to Shaping (*Fig. 6, page 2*).

Back and Leg Edgings

With MC, work same as Basic Crochet.

See **Finishing**, page 2.

14

9. Pink Lady to crochet

SIZE	1	2	3	4	5	6	7	8	9	10	11	12
ounces	1½	2	2½	3	3½	4¾	5¾	6¾	7½	8½	9½	10½
⅝" Ribbon — "	18	18	24	24	30	30	30	30	36	36	36	36
NECK RUFFLE Ch — loosely	42	46	54	64	72	82	96	100	108	118	126	136
Row 1 — loops	20	22	26	31	35	40	47	49	53	58	62	67
Row 2 — loops	19	21	25	30	34	39	46	48	52	57	61	66
Eyelet Row — tr	21	23	27	32	36	41	48	50	54	59	63	68
BODY Row 1 — times more	5	6	7	9	10	12	13	15	16	18	19	21
— time	1	0	1	0	1	0	1	0	0	0	1	0
— V-Sts	14	15	18	21	24	27	30	33	36	39	42	45
Row 2 — times	2	4	6	8	8	10	10	12	12	14	14	16
LEG OPENINGS First Side Row 1 unworked	1	1	1	1	2	2	2	3	3	3	4	4
— V-Sts	2	2	2	2	3	3	3	4	4	4	5	5
Row 2 — times	1	1	1	1	1	1	3	3	3	3	3	3
Center Row 1 skip — V-Sts	1	1	2	2	2	2	3	3	3	3	3	3
work V-St in next — V-St	7	8	9	12	13	16	17	18	21	24	25	28
leave remaining — V-Sts	8	9	10	13	14	17	18	19	22	25	26	29
Row 2 — times	1	1	1	1	1	1	3	3	3	3	3	3

MATERIALS

Worsted Weight Yarn, approximately:

_____ ounces

Crochet hook, size G (4.50 mm) **or** size needed for gauge

⅝" Ribbon - _____ "

¼" Elastic

Yarn needle

GAUGE: 6 V-Sts and 9 rows = 4"

NECK RUFFLE

Ch _____ loosely.

Row 1 (Right side): Sc in second ch from hook, (ch 3, skip next ch, sc in next ch) across: _____ loops.

Note: Loop a short piece of yarn around any stitch to mark last row as **right** side.

Row 2: Turn; slip st in first loop, ch 1, sc in same loop, (ch 4, sc in next loop) across: _____ loops.

Row 3: Turn; slip st in first loop, ch 1, sc in same loop, (ch 5, sc in next loop) across, slip st in same loop; working in end of rows, (slip st in end of next sc and in end of next loop) twice, slip st in first ch of beginning ch.

Eyelet Row: Ch 5 **(counts as first tr plus ch 1)**, working in free loops of beginning ch, skip next ch, tr in next ch, (ch 1, skip next ch, tr in next ch) across: _____ tr.

BODY

Row 1: Ch 4 **(counts as first dc plus ch 1, now and throughout)**, turn; dc in first ch-1 sp, ★ skip next tr, (dc, ch 1, dc) in next tr **(V-St made)**, skip next ch-1 sp, work V-St in next ch-1 sp; repeat from ★ _____ times **more**, work V-St in last tr _____ time; _____ V-Sts.

Row 2: Ch 4, turn; dc in first ch-1 sp, work V-St in next V-St (ch-1 sp) and in each V-St across.

Repeat Row 2, _____ times.

LEG OPENINGS

First Side

Row 1: Ch 4, turn; dc in first ch-1 sp, work V-St in next _____ V-Sts, leave remaining V-Sts unworked: _____ V-Sts.

Row 2: Ch 4, turn; dc in first ch-1 sp, work V-St in next V-St and in each V-St across.

Repeat Row 2, _____ times.

Finish off.

Center

Row 1: With **right** side facing, skip _____ V-Sts from First Side, join yarn with slip st in next V-St; ch 4, dc in same sp, work V-St in next _____ V-St in next V-St and in each V-St across.

Row 2: Ch 4, turn; dc in first ch-1 sp, work V-St in next V-St and in each V-St across.

Repeat Row 2, _____ times.

Finish off.

SIZE	1	2	3	4	5	6	7	8	9	10	11	12
	1	1	2	2	2	2	3	3	3	3	3	3
	2	2	2	2	3	3	3	4	4	4	5	5
	1	1	1	1	1	1	3	3	3	3	3	3
	3	3	6	6	6	6	9	9	9	9	9	9
	3	3	6	6	6	6	9	9	9	9	9	9
	12	13	14	17	20	23	24	27	30	33	36	39
	14	15	18	21	24	27	30	33	36	39	42	45
	4½	5½	6½	7½	8½	9½	10½	11½	12	12½	13	13
	6	6	9	12	12	15	15	15	18	18	21	21
	9	10	11	12	15	16	19	22	23	26	27	30
	10	11	12	13	16	17	20	23	24	27	28	31
	8	9	10	11	14	15	18	21	22	25	26	29
	9	11	13	15	17	19	21	22	23	24	25	26

Second Side

Row 1: With **right** side facing, skip ____ V-Sts from Center, join yarn with slip st in next V-St; ch 4, dc in same sp, work V-St in next V-St and in each V-St across: ____ V-Sts.

Row 2: Ch 4, turn; dc in first ch-1 sp, work V-St in next V-St and in each V-St across.

Repeat Row 2, ____ times.

Closing Row: Ch 4, turn; dc in first ch-1 sp, work V-St in each V-St across Second Side, ch ____ **loosely**, work V-St in each V-St across Center, ch ____ **loosely**, work V-St in each V-St across First Side: ____ V-Sts.

Chest

Row 1: Ch 4, turn; dc in first ch-1 sp, work V-St in next V-St and in each V-St across First Side, skip first ch, work V-St in next ch, (skip next 2 chs, work V-St in next ch) across to last ch, work V-St in each V-St across Center, skip first ch, work V-St in next ch, (skip next 2 chs, work V-St in next ch) across to last ch, work V-St in each V-St across Second Side: ____ V-Sts.

Row 2: Ch 4, turn; dc in first ch-1 sp, work V-St in next V-St and in each V-St across First Side:

Work even until piece measures approximately ____ " from Eyelet Row **or** until desired length to end of rib cage.

Shaping

Row 1: Turn, slip st in first ____ sts, ch 3, work V-St in next ____ V-Sts, work V-St decrease as follows: dc in next V-St, ch 1, YO, pull up a loop in same V-St, YO and draw through 2 loops on hook, YO, pull up a loop in next V-St, YO and draw through 2 loops on hook, YO and draw through all 3 loops on hook **(V-St decrease made)**, leave remaining sts unworked: ____ V-Sts.

Row 2: Ch 4, turn; dc in same V-St, work V-St in next V-St and in each V-St across.

Row 3: Ch 3, work V-St in next V-St and in each V-St across to last 2 V-Sts, work V-St decrease: ____ V-Sts.

Work even until Sweater measures approximately ____ " from Eyelet Row **or** until desired length to base of tail.

Finish off.

Weave seam from Eyelet Row to Shaping (**Fig. 6, page 2**).

Back Edging

Rnd 1: With **right** side and seam facing, join yarn with slip st in first ch-1 sp to the left of seam; ch 1, sc in same sp, ch 3, sc in space **between** next 2 dc, ch 3, (sc in next ch-1 sp, ch 3, sc in sp **between** next 2 dc) across to Shaping; working in end of rows, (sc, ch 3) in each row; working across last row of Sweater, (sc, ch 3) twice in first V-St, sc in sp **between** next 2 dc, ch 3, (sc in next ch-1 sp, ch 3, sc in sp **between** next 2 dc, ch 3) across to last ch-1 sp, (sc, ch 3) twice in last ch-1 sp; working in end of rows, (sc, ch 3) in each row across; sc in sp **between** next 2 dc, ch 3, sc in sp **between** next 2 dc, ch 3) across, sc in seam, ch 3; join with slip st to first sc.

Rnd 2: Slip st in first loop, ch 1, sc in same loop, ch 3, (sc in next loop, ch 3) around; join with slip st to first sc, finish off.

Leg Edging

Rnd 1: With **right** side facing, join yarn with slip st in any V-St of Leg Opening; ch 1, sc in same st, ch 3, (sc in next st, ch 3) around; join with slip st to first sc, finish off. Repeat for second Leg Opening.

See **Finishing**, page 2.

16

10. Grannies to crochet

SIZE	1	2	3	4	5	6	7	8	9	10	11	12
MC (Ecru) - ounces	1	1	1¼	1¾	2¼	3	3½	4	4¾	5	6	7
CC (Scraps) - ounces total	¾	¾	1	1¼	1½	1¾	2	2¼	2¾	3	3¾	4
SQUARE MOTIF (Make)	21	23	29	40	49	67	77	88	99	150	117	134
FILL-IN MOTIF (Make)	1	1	1	2	2	2	3	3	4	4	5	5

MATERIALS

Worsted Weight Yarn, approximately:
MC (Ecru) - _____ ounces
CC (Scraps) - _____ ounces **total**
Crochet hook, size H (5.00 mm) **or size needed for gauge**
Yarn needle
¼" Elastic
Elastic thread

GAUGE: One Square Motif = 2"

SQUARE MOTIF (Make _____)

With CC ch 4, join with slip st to form a ring.
Rnd 1 (Right side): Ch 2, 2 hdc in ring, ch 1, (3 hdc, ch 1) 3 times in ring; join with slip st to first st, finish off: 12 sts.
Note: Loop a short piece of yarn around any stitch to mark last round as **right** side.
Rnd 2: With **right** side facing, join MC with slip st in any ch-1 sp; ch 2, (2 hdc, ch 1, 3 hdc) in same sp, ch 1, (3 hdc, ch 1) twice in each ch-1 sp around; join with slip st to top of beginning ch-2, finish off: 24 sts.

FILL-IN MOTIF (Make _____)

Work same as Square Motif; do **not** finish off.
Row 1: Slip st in next 2 hdc and in next ch-1 sp, ch 1, sc in same sp, (sc in next 3 hdc, sc in next ch-1 sp) twice: 9 sc.
Rows 2-4: Ch 1, turn; pull up a loop in first 2 sc, YO and draw through all 3 loops on hook, sc in each sc across to last 2 sc, pull up a loop in last 2 sc, YO and draw through all 3 loops on hook: 3 sc.
Row 5: Ch 1, turn; skip first sc, pull up a loop in next 2 sc, YO and draw through all 3 loops on hook; finish off.

ASSEMBLY

Referring to the diagram for your size, page 18, whipstitch motifs together (*Fig. 9*).
Matching ●, whipstitch seams together.
On sizes 4-12, matching ○, whipstitch seams together.
On sizes 7-12, matching ▶, whipstitch seams together.
Whipstitch final seam.
If Sweater length needs to be adjusted, add square motifs to back edge.

Fig. 9

With **wrong** sides together, insert yarn needle from **right** to **left** through **front** loop of first square and **back** loop of second square (*Fig. 9*). Bring needle around and insert it from **right** to **left** through the next loops on both pieces. Continue in

17